New ANIMAL Discoveries

Ronald Orenstein

Foreword by Jane Goodall

The Millbrook Press Brookfield, Connecticut

For Randy and Jenny

Published in 2001 by The Millbrook Press, Inc.
2 Old New Milford Road, Brookfield, Connecticut 06804
www.millbrookpress.com

First published in Canada in 2001 by Key Porter Books Limited
70 The Esplanade
Toronto, Ontario
Canada M5E 1R2
www.keyporter.com

The Library of Congress Control Number: 00-050003
ISBN 0-7613-2274-4 (lib. bdg.)

Photo Credits:
Page 7 © The Jane Goodall Institute; Page 9 © Petra Ehresmann; Page 11 © Amy Lathrop/Royal Ontario Museum; Page 13 © Marc Erdmann; Page 14 © M. Lammertink; Page 17 © Neptune Aquarium; Page 18 © John Cann; Page 19 © Ed Smith; Page 20 © Ed Smith; Page 21 © Lars Dinesen; Page 22 © Lars Dinesen; Page 24 © Tim Flannery/Australian Museum; Page 25 © Tim Flannery/Australian Museum; Page 26 © John MacKinnon; Page 27 © John MacKinnon; Page 28 © World Wildlife Fund, John MacKinnon; Page 29 (upper and lower) © William Robichaud; Page 30 © John MacKinnon; Page 31 © William Robichaud; Page 32 © William Robichaud; Page 33 © John MacKinnon; Page 34 © Alan Rabinowitz/ Wildlife Conservation Society; Page 37 © Maurizio Dioli; Page 38 (left and right) © Maurizio Dioli; Page 39 © Maurizio Dioli; Page 41 (left and right) © David Haring; Page 43 © Kenneth E. Glander; Page 44 © Kenneth E. Glander; Page 46 © Zig Koch; Page 47 © Mauricio de Almeida Noronha/Brazil Conservation International; Page 48 (left) © R. H. Mittermeier/Brazil Conservation International; Page 48 (middle) © Marc Van Roosmalen; Page 48 (right) © Marc Van Roosmalen; Page 51 © Julio Reyes; Page 52 © Julio Reyes; Page 53 © Nan Hauser/Hoyt Peckham; Page 54 (top) © Reinhardt Møbjerg Kristensen; Page 54 (bottom) © R.P. Higgins; Page 55 © Gerda Møbjerg Kristensen; Page 57 © Reinhardt Møbjerg Kristensen; Page 58 © Reinhardt Møbjerg Kristensen; Page 62 © Nan Hauser/Hoyt Peckham.

Design: Peter Maher
Electronic formatting: Jean Lightfoot Peters

00 01 02 03 6 5 4 3 2 1

Printed and bound in Singapore

Acknowledgments

No one could write a book like this without help. I am very grateful to John Cann, Noël Dilly, Lars Dinesen, Maurizio Dioli, Petra Ehresmann, Marc Erdmann and Arnaz Mehta Erdmann, Tim Flannery, Robert Higgins, Reinhardt Kristensen, John MacKinnon, James Mead, Alan Rabinowitz, Julio Reyes, Edmund Smith, Ian Tattersall, Koen Van Waerebeek and Patricia Wright for answering my questions, and providing me with information and pictures. I also had help from Kenneth Glander and Elwyn Simons of Duke University, Ella Outlaw and Conservation International, and William Robichaud and the Wildlife Conservation Society. Thanks also to Carlos Alvarez, Alan Baker Sr., Susan Baker, Matt Bille, Peter Bryant, Roy L. Caldwell, James V. Carretta, Abigail Caudron, Harold Cogger, Ronald E. Cole, Loren Coleman, Rosamond Kidman Cox, Lesa Davis, Karen Dickson, Linda Dunn, Joe Erwin, Steve Ferrari, Pieter Folkens, Birute Galdikas, Don Glasco, Lisa Gould, Nan Hauser, John E. Heyning, David Hulse, Stephen Leatherwood, John M. Legler, Colin D. MacLeod, Shirley McGreal, John Campbell McNamara, Michel C. Milinkovitch, Steve Mirsky, Darren Naish, Stephen Nash, George Olshevsky, Daniel M. Palacios, Jose Truda Palazzo, Paula Pebsworth, Patricia Petiet, Bob Pitman, Michel Raynal, Ian Redmond, Ben Roesch, Noel Rowe, Mario Salinas, Nikolaj Scharff, Bill Sellers, Jessica Speart, Mary Beth Voltura, Vern Weitzel and Bettina Wurche for advice, information and comments along the way. Also thanks to my editors at Key Porter Books, Michael Mouland, Derek Weiler and Andrea Bock. Special "thank yous" to Simon Conway Morris for allowing me to quote him in this book and to Vera Zietemann for getting up out of a sickbed to show me the golden-brown mouse lemur in Madagascar. Finally, my very special thanks to Jane Goodall, for her friendship, her advice, her lovely Foreword, and everything she has done for people and animals new and old throughout her career.

ARCTIC OCEAN

Greenland

Page 53

Iceland

Page 56

Norway

Denmark

Page 53

United Kingdom

Canada

Europe

MEDITERRANEAN SEA

USA

NORTH ATLANTIC OCEAN

Mexico

GULF OF MEXICO

Tropic of Cancer

Africa

Ethiopia

Kenya

Somali Re

GULF OF GUINEA

Equator

PACIFIC OCEAN

Peru

Amazon Forest

Brazil

Lima

Tanzania

Comoros

Madagascar

P.

Page 22

Tropic of Capricorn

Page 51

São Paulo

Curitiba

Superagüi

MATA ATLANTICA

Page 46

SOUTH ATLANTIC OCEAN

Chile

SOUTHERN OCEAN

Antarctica

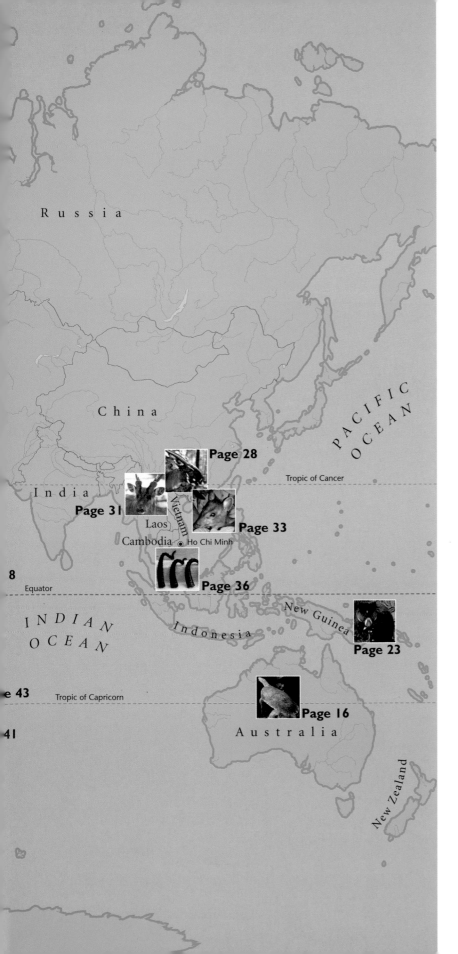

Contents

Foreword

When I was growing up, 50 years ago, reading books about wild animals, I envied the early naturalists who came back from their travels with tales of unknown animals. I remember reading about the first reports of the mysterious okapi, the pygmy hippo and many other fascinating creatures. "How sad," I thought, "there will be no new animals to discover when I am grown up." But I was wrong! Since I was a child all sorts of amazing animals have been discovered—by naturalists and scientists that is; the indigenous people knew about them all along.

Just a few years ago, when I was in Brazil, I was one of the very first scientists to see a dwarf marmoset, a tiny monkey that had only just been discovered. It was so exciting! Especially when the tiny creature took food from my hand, then jumped onto my shoulder.

This book tells about some of the wonderful animals that have recently been discovered. And there are more unknown creatures out there in the wild places of the world. The trouble is, humans are destroying those wild places very fast. If we want to learn about the behavior of these newly discovered animals we must work much harder to save their habitats or it

Dr. Jane Goodall has spent her life studying wild chimpanzees and working to save them from extinction.

will be too late. And some of the animals that are still unknown to science will become extinct even before we discover them. Many have gone already.

Ron Orenstein is devoting his life to trying to save wild animals in their wild homes. My colleagues and I are trying to protect chimpanzees, the species that I have been learning about for more than 35 years. To protect them we must protect the forests where they live. And when we protect a forest, we protect all the amazing varieties of creatures that live there—including those not yet identified. I hope that you will help us; otherwise we shall fail.

Jane Goodall

The Age of Discovery

he little creature stared at me with big round eyes. It looked like a tiny, fuzzy elf with pointed ears and orange-tawny fur. I stared back.

I was in Madagascar, the great island off Africa's eastern coast. It was July 1997. The animal I was watching had no scientific name. Until a few months before my visit, scientists had not even realized it existed. It was a new species.

My little elf did not get its official scientific name until months later. Today it is known as the golden-brown mouse lemur, *Microcebus ravelobensis*.

New Animal Discoveries is about animals that scientists have discovered in the last two decades. These animals received their scientific names—the final step scientists take to announce their discoveries—after 1983 (the year my son, Randy, was born). Most had to wait until after 1987 (the year my daughter, Jenny, was born). Some—like the little animal I met in Madagascar—were even discovered *while* this book was being written.

Discoveries have been made in lots of surprising places. Some new species live in remote tropical forests, others have turned up in everyday beach sand. New species have been

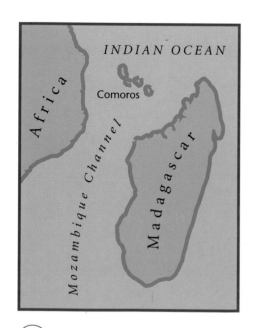

The golden-brown mouse lemur (*Microcebus ravelobensis*) (left) looks very much like the gray mouse lemur (*Microcebus murinus*) (right). That is why it took so long for scientists to realize it was a different species.

discovered in fish markets, for sale in pet shops, even on TV! Discoveries can happen anywhere—maybe even in your own backyard.

Are there really enough newly discovered animals to fill a whole book? Yes! In fact, there are so many, the hardest job has been to decide which ones to write about.

Most of the new discoveries, though, are of insects. Hundreds of new insects are discovered each year. There are probably millions—yes, millions—left to find, particularly in the canopy of tropical rainforests. But there are no insects in this book. There just isn't room for them.

Instead, *New Animal Discoveries* is about kangaroos and partridges, turtles and monkeys, forest oxen, barking deer, microscopic girdle-wearers and even a whale or two. It's about a whole range of beautiful, strange and fascinating creatures whose very existence proves that the world is richer than we had imagined it to be. Richer—and more precious.

TV Program Reveals New Species!

In 1994, British scientists watching a nature program on the Andes of southern Ecuador noticed a mouse with dense, woolly fur. It was a fishing mouse, a South American rodent that hunts for fish and small water animals with a mass of sensitive whiskers. But no fishing mouse was known where the program was filmed.

Zoologist Adrian Burnett realized that the mouse matched unidentified specimens he had collected in the early 1980s. In 1998, he described the Andean fishing mouse, *Chibchanomys orcesi*. It lives on a single plateau 13,123 feet (4,000 meters) above sea level, where it may be endangered.

Species, Names and Specimens

What is a species?

Species is Latin for "appearance," but whether two animals belong to the same species or to different species is not really based on what they look like. Some animals of different species look alike; some animals of the same species look very different. A chihuahua and a great dane, for example, both belong to the same species—domestic dogs—but they don't look very much alike. What really makes a group of animals a species is their ability to breed freely with each other. Animals that belong to the same species breed together, animals that belong to different species usually can't do that.

What are scientific names?

Every living thing that is recognized by scientists has to have a *scientific name*. Names like *Homo sapiens* (the name we give ourselves) or *Tyrannosaurus rex* are examples of scientific names. Scientific names were invented over 250 years ago, in the 1730s, by a Swedish botanist named Karl von Linné. In Linné's day, the language of science was Latin, which was understood by educated people throughout the Western world no matter what their own language might be. Many scientists even turned their own names into Latin; Linné himself is much better known by his Latin name, Carolus Linnaeus. Even today, scientific names are usually in Latin or Greek.

Thinking up new names can be tricky. Scientists who study insects discover so many new species that name hunting can get a bit silly. Maybe that's why there are wasps named *Polemistus chewbacca* and *Polemistus yoda*!

How does the Linnaean system work?

Double-barreled scientific names like *Homo sapiens* place each species within a system, invented by Linnaeus, that explains how we think living creatures are related to each other. It works like this:

The species *sapiens* (that's us) belongs to the genus *Homo* (which includes extinct humans, like Neanderthals), which belongs to the family *Hominidae* (humans and other extinct apelike animals), which belongs to the order Primates (humans, plus lemurs, apes and monkeys), which is part of a class, the Mammalia or mammals (everything from whales to elephants), which fits in the phylum (pronounced *fie'*-lum) Chordata (mammals, fishes, amphibians, reptiles, birds, etc.), which is one of the major divisions of the animal kingdom.

What is a type specimen?

You can't name a new species until you have a specimen. In fact, the rules that govern scientific names state that anyone naming a new species has to pick, and describe, at least one specimen that "officially" carries the scientific name. The specimen is called a *type specimen*. That is because museums may have many specimens of an animal, all supposed to be of the same species. What if it turns out in the future that some of them really belong to a different species? Which set of specimens gets the original scientific name?

The type specimen rule solves that problem. If the species is ever split into two, the name goes with the type specimen and all of the animals like it; the others have to be given a new name. In fact, one of the others has to be picked to be the type specimen that goes with the new name!

Do we really need specimens?

Collecting a specimen almost always means killing it, so its remains can be preserved in a museum (if it isn't already dead—fossil collectors don't have this problem!). This bothers a lot of people, including a few scientists. But collecting is absolutely necessary, and not just so that other scientists can have something to study.

Many new species are rare. That is why they are so hard to find. They may need protection urgently. The people who can make the decisions that are needed to help them survive—lawmakers, for example—may ask for proof that there really is something to protect. A specimen, properly labeled, provides that proof. Collecting may help save the lives of the rest of its species and of many other animals besides.

What Is a New Species?

There's nothing really "new" about new species. Like new friends, new species have been around long before we met them; we just didn't know it. When I say "we," I really mean zoologists, the scientists who study animals.

A species may be new to scientists, but that doesn't mean that nobody knew it existed. Sometimes the scientist who discovers a new species really is the first person to see it, particularly if the animal is very tiny or has been hauled up from the depths of the sea. But many "newly discovered" creatures have been known for centuries to the people who live where the animals do. "New" really means "new to science."

This peculiar-looking toad (*Bufo galeatus*) is only one of many new discoveries from Vietnam.

Imagine you have just discovered a new species. Then what?

To make the species officially "known to science," you have to *describe* it. In order to do that, you first need a specimen. A photograph won't do. You don't need the whole animal—many fossil animals are known only from a bit of bone or tooth—but you must have enough of a specimen to prove that the animal really is new. Many new species—like the golden-brown mouse lemur—look very similar to their closest relatives. You may need to spend hours comparing your specimen with other specimens in museums, or reading technical articles in the library.

When you are sure your species is new, you can choose a scientific name for it, in Latin or Greek. Make sure that no one has used your name before: no two animal species can have the same scientific name.

The next step is to announce your discovery to the scientific world. You need to write a paper. This is called the *description*. First you describe your species in detail. Then you announce its name. You also discuss how you think your species is related to other animals and perhaps talk about how it evolved, where it lives, what its behavior is like and anything else you have learned. Finally, you send your paper to a scientific journal like *Nature* or *Science*, where it will be sent to other scientists, who review it to see if it is accurate before it is published.

Why do you need a description if you already have a specimen?

First you have to prove to other scientists that your species really is new. For the species in this book that isn't a problem, because most of them are very different from even their closest

Arnaz Mehta Erdmann swims alongside a new species of coelacanth (*Latimeria menadoensis*). She and her husband Marc discovered this remarkable fish in Sulawesi, Indonesia in 1997.

relatives. But many new species may be only slightly different, and you must make sure that those differences are real.

Other scientists, though, may not be able to examine your specimen for themselves; they will have to read about it. That's why you need to write a description, and if you want other scientists to accept your claim that your species is new, you will have to make sure that your description contains enough details to convince them.

Discovery can be a lot of work!

The world's smallest frog: *Eleutherodactylus iberia* sits on a Cuban coin. The coin is the size of an American nickel.

Twentieth-century Surprises

New species have been making headlines for years. In 1901, while tracking a mysterious African forest "horse," the explorer Sir Harry Johnstone discovered the okapi *(Okapia johnstonei),* which is really a short-necked giraffe. In 1976, newspapers printed photographs of the first megamouth *(Megachasma pelagios),* a 14-foot-long (4.3-meter-long) flabby-bodied, round-nosed shark that cruises the deep waters of the world sweeping tiny sea creatures into its gaping jaws.

It's not every day that a fish makes the front page, but one that turned up in 1936, in a fisherman's net off the coast of South Africa, was no ordinary fish. It was 6 feet (1.8 meters) long and bright blue, with heavy plated scales, fleshy fins and a mouth like a bulldog's. To the amazement of scientists everywhere, it was a coelacanth (pronounced *seel*-a-canth). Coelacanths were supposed to have vanished with the dinosaurs 65 million years ago! What's more, the coelacanth is the only living member of the group of fishes that gave rise to amphibians, reptiles, birds and mammals (including people). The coelacanth *(Latimeria chalumnae)* is probably our closest living fish cousin.

Coelacanths made headlines again in 1998. For decades scientists thought that coelacanths lived only around the Comoro Islands, in the western Indian Ocean. In 1997, however, Dr. Marc Erdmann and his wife, Arnaz, were celebrating their honeymoon on the Indonesian island of Sulawesi, 6,200 miles (9,977 kilometers) east of the Comoros, when Arnaz spotted a dead coelacanth going by on a fisherman's cart. In July 1998, they found another, this one alive—enough to prove that a second species of coelacanth (*Latimeria menadoensis*) lives around Sulawesi. The local fishermen knew it all the time, of course. They called it "*rajah laut*," king of the sea.

Record-breaking Discoveries

Some twentieth-century discoveries have made the record books:

1904—*The World's Largest Pig*: The giant forest hog (*Hylochoerus meinertzhageni*) of central Africa.

1907—*The World's Largest Butterfly*: Queen Alexandra's birdwing (*Ornithoptera alexandrae*) of New Guinea, brought down by a shotgun blast, of all things.

1912—*The World's Largest Lizard*: The Komodo dragon (*Varanus komodoensis*) of Indonesia.

1930—*One of the World's Largest Freshwater Fish*: The pa beuk, or Mekong giant catfish (*Pangasianodon gigas*), of southeast Asia.

1973—*The World's Smallest Mammal*: The bumblebee bat (*Crasseonycteris thonglongyai*) of Thailand.

1996—*The World's Smallest Frog*: A tiny frog from Cuba (*Eleutherodactylus iberia*), which is actually tied for this title with another frog, from Brazil.

From Forest and Mountain

A famous scientist once said that all the birds in the world had been discovered. He had to eat his words: we are still discovering two or three new species every year. You can read about two of them here, both from East Africa. With them are the stories of a turtle from Australia and a very peculiar kangaroo. Though you might think that new turtles and new kangaroos would be hard to find, the two in this book are not even the only ones to be discovered in the 1990s! Surely there are still plenty of wonderful discoveries to be made.

Found in a Drum

The Mary River Turtle (*Elusor macrurus*)

In the late 1950s and early 1960s, thousands of peculiar-looking baby turtles began showing up in pet shops around Australia. John Cann knew his turtles, but he didn't recognize these, and he didn't know where they came from. Though he traveled great distances on one wild-goose chase after another, it took Cann 25 years to find out.

Cann's luck turned in 1990, when a man in Maryborough, in the subtropical Australian state of Queensland, sent him a note saying, "I've got one!" Cann dashed to Maryborough only to find that the turtle, swimming in a water-filled metal drum on his host's property, was a perfectly ordinary one. Cann was furious until his host said, "Well, if that's not him, let's have a look in this drum"—and there was Cann's mystery turtle, a full-grown female.

John Cann christened it the Mary River turtle *(Elusor macrurus)*. Its scientific name, roughly translated, means "the hard-to-find animal with the big tail." It turned out to be the largest freshwater turtle in Australia. Its shell is approximately 15.6 inches (40 centimeters) long. Males have a long, heavy tail

The Mary River turtle takes its scientific name, *Elusor macrurus*, from its large, heavy tail. *"Macrurus"* means "big-tailed."

as thick as a human wrist. It is the biggest tail on any turtle, much bigger than its head and neck. Like most Australian turtles, the Mary River turtle cannot pull its head into its shell; it tucks it in sideways.

Cann may have found his turtle just in time, because *Elusor macrurus* is an endangered species, though Australian scientists are busy studying ways to save it. As far as we know, the only place it lives is in deep pools along 62 miles (99.8 kilometers) of the middle reaches of the Mary River, south of Maryborough. It lays its eggs in nests on the river's sandy banks. Unfortunately, many forces threaten its habitat. People like to visit these sandy banks. So do cattle, which come down to the river to drink. In time, a bank or sandbar can be trampled out of existence, leaving the turtles no place to nest. Foxes—an animal introduced to Australia from the United Kingdom—steal eggs from the turtles' nests. Nearby farming and mining pollutes the river water where the turtles live.

By the way, baby turtles don't really make good pets. Most of the turtles you see in pet shops have been taken from the wild, just like the Mary River turtles were. Not only are they being removed from their natural habitat, but it isn't easy to keep a turtle healthy. Many of them die before they even get to the shop or within a few months of their arrival. Wild turtles should be left in the wild.

The Discoverer's Dilemma

The Bulo Burti Bush-shrike (*Laniarius liberatus*)

In order to describe a new species properly, you have to collect a *type specimen* (see page 10). That usually means that you have to either kill the animal or keep it until it dies, and then preserve its remains in a museum.

But what if your discovery is so rare that if you collect even one, you could cause the extinction of the species? Should you forget about it? And what if announcing your discovery is the only way to provide the protection it needs to survive?

In August 1988, Edmund Smith was visiting a patch of woodland in the town of Bulo Burti, Somalia, in northeastern Africa. He saw a bird he could not identify. It was a bush-shrike, one of a group of colorful African birds with loud, beautiful songs. But it did not match any known species.

Smith decided not to kill the bird. Instead, in January 1989,

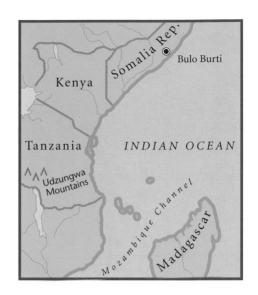

The only Bulo Burti Bush-shrike any scientist has ever seen is free again in the woodlands of Somalia.

The Bulo Burti Bush-shrike was the first bird to have been described from DNA and tissue samples, and then set free.

Somali scientist Osman Gedow Amir trapped the bird. Then Amir and Smith photographed it, videotaped it and recorded its calls. You cannot use a recording or a photograph as a type specimen, however, so Smith and Amir also saved some feathers and took blood samples. Two Danish scientists, Peter Arctander and Jon Fjeldså, then extracted DNA from the bird's blood and analyzed it. The blood samples, feathers and DNA gave the four scientists enough specimen material to give the bird a scientific name. They planned to set it free, so they named it *Laniarius liberatus*, "the freed one."

Unfortunately, setting the bird free turned out to be more difficult than they'd imagined. Civil war had broken out in Somalia, so Smith took the bird to Germany, where it lived in a

The only home of the Udzungwa forest partridge covers less than 116 square miles (300 square kilometers) of this forest in the Udzungwa Mountains, Tanzania.

cage for more than a year. By the time the bird could be returned to Somalia, the woodland around Bulo Burti had been destroyed. Smith and his colleagues took it to a nature reserve as close to Bulo Burti as they could get. There, after a week spent in an open-air cage getting used to the area, the bird was set free.

Was all this effort worth it? Many scientists don't think so. Some argue that after living in captivity for so long, the bird probably wouldn't have been able to survive in the wild anyway, especially in a new area. Others say that if collecting a single specimen would drive the bird to extinction, the species was probably doomed anyway, so it would be better for science to retain the whole specimen.

Though the beautifully-patterned Udzungwa forest partridge lives in Africa, its nearest relatives are in Asia.

No scientist has seen a Bulo Burti Bush-shrike since the bird was set free. Perhaps it is extinct, perhaps not. Was Smith showing how scientists ought to behave when they discover a new species? Or was he letting his feelings get in the way of doing a proper job of discovery?

What do *you* think?

A Stranger in Africa

The Udzungwa Forest Partridge
(*Xenoperdix udzungwensis*)

In eastern Tanzania, Africa, between the Indian Ocean and the great flat plains of the Serengeti, lie a series of low, scattered mountain ranges topped with evergreen forest. Many of the animals and plants that inhabit this region live nowhere else.

That is why Lars Dinesen of the Zoological Museum at the University of Copenhagen found himself in the Udzungwa Mountains in July 1991. Dinesen already knew about some of the special creatures of the Udzungwas. The beautiful little rufous-winged sunbird (*Nectarinia rufipennis*) had been discovered there just 10 years earlier.

On July 3, Dinesen came across a small flock of partridges (ground birds related to chickens and peacocks). He knew they were unusual, but he didn't know how unusual until he compared specimens of this new partridge with others in museums. There are many kinds of African partridges (or *francolin*), but strangely, this partridge's nearest relations did not seem to be in Africa at all, but in tropical Asia.

The Udzungwas

On the ancient, rain-soaked Udzungwa, Usumbara and Uluguru Mountains of eastern Africa live animals and plants found nowhere else in the world and others only found thousands of miles away in western Africa. Because the mountains have been almost untouched for millions of years, they have had a long time to be colonized by animals and plants from distant regions. Once the animals and plants arrived, many of them evolved into something unique. People have carried one East African mountain specialty around the world. You might even have one growing in your house: *Saintpaulia ionantha*, the African violet.

How did an Asian bird end up in the Udzungwa Mountains? Thirty million years ago, during the Miocene period, rainforests stretched from west Africa to the Far East. At that time there was no Red Sea, and no Sahara or Arabian Desert. Before the deserts spread and the Red Sea opened, a few Asian animals were able to make the trek from Asia to Africa. Their descendants, like the Udzungwa forest partridge, are still there.

Dinesen named his discovery *Xenoperdix udzungwensis*, "the strange partridge from Udzungwa." He didn't mean that the bird was strange, only that it was a "stranger" in Africa.

When Dinesen returned to the Udzungwa Mountains in 1995, the partridges were still there, shepherding their broods of chicks through the forest. The discovery of the partridges may help ensure that they stay in the forest. Until 1994, there was some logging in the Udzungwas, but this has since stopped. Dinesen is now working to have the range of the partridge included in the Udzungwa Mountains National Park. This will protect the birds, their forest home and all the other creatures that live there.

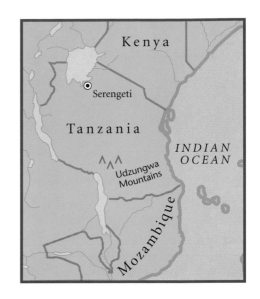

A Panda with a Pouch?

The Dingiso (*Dendrolagus mbaiso*)

When the hunter stepped out of the mist, Dr. Tim Flannery thought for a moment that the animal slung over his shoulder was some sort of panda. But pandas live in China, and Dr. Flannery was in the mountains of western New Guinea. The hunter was carrying a tree-kangaroo. The year was 1994, and science was finally meeting the dingiso.

New Guinea

New Guinea, over 1,000 miles (2,200 kilometers) long, sits atop northern Australia like a giant bird. Exploring its rugged mountains and steep valleys is difficult and sometimes dangerous. But zoologists still go to study its mammals, insects, frogs and birds.

New Guinea's most famous animals are the birds of paradise. Thirty-six of the forty-two species live nowhere else. Their dazzling plumes are worn as ornaments by New Guinea peoples. The first bird of paradise skins to reach Europe, centuries ago, had no feet. This gave rise to a legend that the birds lived in heaven, or paradise, where they never landed, feeding on air.

Scientists did not see a living dingiso, a black-and-white, ground-dwelling tree kangaroo from western New Guinea, until 1994.

Tree-kangaroos live in the rainforests of New Guinea and northern Australia. They look like a cross between a giant raccoon, an overweight monkey and a teddy bear. They are poor tree climbers, and they escape danger by jumping out of trees onto the ground, sometimes from as high as 64 feet (20 meters). They then bound off into the forest on their powerful legs.

In 1993, Dr. Flannery had purchased a hat from a Dani

hunter that contained a bit of black-and-white fur. It was definitely tree-kangaroo fur, but what kind? A little while later a South African photographer, Gerald Cubitt, sent pictures of a Dani man holding a peculiar black tree-kangaroo with a white chest. What was it? Flannery, the leading expert on New Guinea's mammals, didn't know.

One year later, when Flannery arrived in the Carstensz Mountains of western New Guinea, he found that the local hunters knew all about the mysterious animal. The Dani called it the *wanun*; the Moni called it the *dingiso*, which means "large black game animal." Dani hunters had killed nearly all the dingiso in their area, but some Moni clans considered it to be sacred. They referred to it as *bondegezou*, which means "the man of the alpine forest." They considered it to be their ancestor or *mbaiso*, "the forbidden one." To eat it would be cannibalism.

The Dani and Moni hunters told Dr. Flannery that the dingiso was tame; one hunter caught one simply by walking up to it, putting a rope around its neck and leading it away. When it is frightened, a dingiso will lift its arms, showing its white belly, and whistle (unlike other tree-kangaroos, which grunt).

Although it is a tree-kangaroo, the dingiso hardly ever climbs trees. When it does, it doesn't jump out like its cousins; it shinnies down the trunk backwards, the way we do. The dingiso has become a tree-kangaroo that lives on the ground. Kangaroo ancestors probably lived in trees at one time. So the dingiso's ancestors first lived in trees, then climbed down to become kangaroos, then climbed back up to become tree-kangaroos. Then they finally came back down to become the furry black-and-white "man" that hops through the alpine forest of the Carstensz Mountains.

Dr. Tim Flannery

Tim Flannery is well known in Australia as a scientist, a best-selling writer and a radio commentator. His book about the environment, *The Future Eaters*, was made into an Australian television series.

Dr. Flannery studied English at university before moving on to study palaeontology and zoology. Today, he is Principal Research Scientist at the Australian Museum. He has been studying the mammals of New Guinea for nearly 20 years. The dingiso is just one of his discoveries.

Southeast Asia's Lost World

here really is a Lost World. It has been cut off from the rest of the world perhaps for millions of years. You won't find *Tyrannosaurus rex* there, but it is full of amazing animals unknown to the outside world until only a few years ago.

The real Lost World lies in Southeast Asia, on the border of Laos and Vietnam, where the Annamite Mountains rise over 6,560 feet (2,000 meters) above sea level. Moist winds rising from the South China Sea drench the mountain slopes with

Many newly-discovered species live in the dense mountain forests of the Vu Quang Reserve, Vietnam.

rain and cloak them in fog. They water an almost impenetrable rainforest. The forest is swelteringly hot and humid. Its trails are rugged, steep and covered with slippery mud. Malaria mosquitoes and bloodsucking leeches wait for passersby. And on top of all that, for many years wars in Vietnam and Laos made it impossible for scientists even to set foot in this place.

In 1992, Dr. John MacKinnon and a team of Vietnamese scientists, funded by the World Wildlife Fund, departed on an expedition to the Vu Quang (pronounced *voo kwong*) Nature Reserve on the Vietnamese side of the mountains. MacKinnon had decided to explore the Vu Quang after looking at satellite photographs. He had no idea what to expect.

What he found, on his first day in the forest, amazed the world.

Southeast Asia's Lost World: the forests of the Annamite Mountains on the border between Laos and Vietnam, home to many newly-discovered species.

John MacKinnon

British zoologist John MacKinnon has spent the last three decades studying the animals of Asia, and finding ways to protect them. He was one of the first scientists to follow wild orangutans through the jungles of Borneo. Dr MacKinnon spent more than seven years in and around Borneo, and eight years in China. He heads a group of experts that advises the Chinese government on ways to protect its wildlife.

Today, John MacKinnon lives in the Philippines where he is developing a Regional Center for Biodiversity Conservation to help conserve wild animals, plants and their habitats throughout Southeast Asia.

The Unexpected Ox

The Saola (*Pseudoryx nghetinensis*)

The hunters who live near Vu Quang decorate their huts with skulls of forest animals. In Kim Quang, one of the nearby villages, Dr. MacKinnon and Vietnamese scientist Do Tuoc saw a skull with long straight horns hanging on the wall of a village elder's hut. No known animal in Southeast Asia had horns like that. What creature had the skull come from?

Over the next few weeks the expedition found more horns, skulls and even skins from the strange creature—the first new species of large land mammal to be discovered in over 50 years. The villagers called it saola (pronounced *sow*—rhymes with cow—*lah*), which means "weaving spindle," because its horns looked like their own wooden spindles. In 1994, zoologists Alan Rabinowitz and George Schaller found evidence that the saola lives in Laos too.

The horns of the saola look similar to the horns of an antelope, the oryx, hence its scientific name, *Pseudoryx*, which literally means "false oryx." Nevertheless, the saola may be more closely related to the common ancestor of cattle, goats and sheep than it is to the antelopes. It stands almost 3.3 feet (1 meter) high at the shoulder and weighs up to 220 pounds (100 kilograms). It is a very beautiful animal, rich reddish-brown with white eyebrows, stripes and patches on its face, a white stripe across its rump and white "socks" above its hooves. Perhaps these markings make it hard to see in the dappled light of the forest. The saola has large scent glands on its face, covered with a flap of skin that it can raise like an awning. It probably uses them to scent-mark its territory in the forest.

In 1994, two young saola calves were captured and taken to

Martha, the only adult saola ever kept in captivity, lived for only one month in the tiny zoo in Lak Xao, Laos.

The white markings on the face of the saola, like patches of dappled sunlight, may help it blend in to the depths of the forest.

a botanical garden near Hanoi, Vietnam's capital. These calves were the first living saola to be seen outside the Lost World. Unfortunately, the female lived for only four or five months, the male even less. In January 1996, an adult female, injured by a hunter's dog, was captured in Laos. She was taken to a private zoo in the little town of Lak Xao (pronounced Lak *sow*). Though she appeared to be settling in well, charming everyone with her remarkable tameness, Martha, as she was named, died after only a month.

Vu Quang Village on the edge of the Vu Quang Reserve in Vietnam, where John MacKinnon and his team first found evidence of the saola.

To this day, other than the three captives, no one has seen a living saola except for the native mountain hunters who share its home. In 1998, though, a wild saola took its own picture by triggering a camera trap that scientist Marc Blitzer had hidden in the forest.

In Laos, the Hmong tribesmen call the saola *saht supahb* "polite animal", because it steps slowly and quietly through the forest. They say it is shy and calm. They usually see it on its own or in pairs, and sometimes in little groups of four or five. It haunts the steep, forested mountains, moving up and down the slopes with the seasons. Its hooves are narrow, and concave on the bottom, like suction cups, probably to give the saola a better grip on the slippery ground.

The saola is very rare. There may be only a few hundred of

them. The Hmong people are poor and hungry. They hunt the saola with dogs and snares. Many of them do not know that the saola cannot be found anywhere else in the world, and they could not pass up a meal even if they did. Some hunters have learned that the outside world is interested in the saola and have deliberately tried to trap them alive. This has to stop. But part of the job of protecting the saola, now that we know about it, involves helping the villagers who hunt it to find a better way of life.

Big Barking Deer . . .

The Giant Muntjac (*Megamuntiacus vuquangensis*)

The little zoo in Lak Xao, Laos—the same one that was briefly the home of Martha the saola—also has a pen for barking deer.

A giant muntjac in the zoo at Lak Xao, Laos. In 1994, scientists visiting the zoo realized that this deer belonged to an unknown species.

The antlers of the giant muntjac may not
seem very large, but they are much longer
than those on any barking deer.

Barking deer, or muntjac, are common forest animals in
Southeast Asia. They are small, stocky deer with short antlers
that perch on top of a stalk, or *pedicel*, of bone. They really
do bark, or at least they make a loud, sharp noise that sounds
like a bark.

The animals in the pen at Lak Xao were supposedly the
well-known common muntjac. One of them certainly was. It
was the right size, about 55 pounds (25 kilograms), and had
the reddish-brown coat of the common muntjac. But when
scientists from the Wildlife Conservation Society visited the
zoo in 1994, they found that one of the barking deer looked
peculiar. Its coat was brown and grizzled, its antlers almost
four times as long as the common muntjac's. It was also much
bigger, at 110 pounds (50 kilograms) twice the common
muntjac's weight. What was it?

Zoologists in Vietnam had been asking the same question.
They had found odd-looking skulls with oversized antlers in
the villages near Vu Quang. Finally, only a few weeks before the
visit to the Lak Xao Zoo, they announced that the Vu Quang
held a second surprise: a giant muntjac. They named it

Megamuntiacus vuquangensis, the giant barking deer. The oversized animal in the pen at Lak Xao Zoo was also a giant muntjac. It was the first, and remains the only, living giant muntjac scientists have ever seen. It turns out, however, that a photograph of a pair of giant muntjac antlers—misidentified of course—had been published in a scientific journal back in 1899!

. . . and Little Barking Deer

The Truong Son Muntjac *(Muntiacus truongsonensis)*

In 1997, a team of Vietnamese and international scientists announced that they had discovered another new species of

The Vu Quang Reserve in Vietnam is home to the saola and the giant muntjac.

This leaf deer *(Muntiacus putaoensis)*, from northern Myanmar, was the first pygmy muntjac seen alive by western scientists.

barking deer, almost 250 miles (400 kilometers) southeast of Vu Quang, in the forests along Vietnam's border with Laos. Instead of being a giant, this one was a pygmy. As far as we can tell from the skulls, it is half the size of a common muntjac and one-quarter the size of a giant muntjac. It weighs about 34 pounds (15.4 kilograms) and stands only 14 inches (35 centimeters) high at the shoulder. The new deer has very short antlers: little unbranched spikes only as long as a thumbnail. Its fur is blackish, with long white hairs on the underside of its tail. While other male barking deer have long canine teeth that they use for fighting, the teeth of the pygmy are the same size in both males and females.

Scientists have named this pygmy deer the Truong Son muntjac *(Muntiacus truongsonensis)*. Truong Son (pronounced *jewng sern*) is the Vietnamese name for the Annamite

Protecting the Lost World

The saola and the new muntjacs are not the only wonders the Lost World has to offer. Many of Asia's most endangered species find refuge there: tigers, Asian golden cats, sun bears, Asian elephants, even the extremely rare Sumatran rhinoceros. Two of the world's most endangered monkeys, the douc langur and the Ha Tinh langur, also live in this forest. Over 400 species of birds have been seen in the mountains, including rare and beautiful pheasants and the endangered white-winged duck. No one knows how many lizards, snakes and frogs live there—many of them also new to science.

In 1995, Dr. George Schaller of the Wildlife Conservation Society discovered that the Vietnamese warty pig (*Sus bucculentus*), an animal thought to be extinct for over 100 years, still lives on the Laotian side of the border. In 1996, conservationist Rob Timmins found a new species of short-eared striped rabbit in a food market in Ben Lak, Laos. Its only relative lives on the island of Sumatra, where it may now be extinct. A new species of river carp, *Parazacco vuquangensis*, turned up in 1992, and in 1997 another new fish, called "co" by the local villagers, turned out to be so common in Vu Quang that scientists caught 18 of them in 15 minutes!

But the Lost World, wonderful as it is, is in danger.

Thousands of people live in the mountains of the Lost World, particularly on the Vietnamese side. They hunt the forest animals. Their numbers are growing. They need more and more land to grow their rice, and they cut down the forest to get it.

The outside world is threatening the forest too. Logging companies want to cut down its trees for timber. In Laos there are plans to build a road right through the forest into Vietnam and a huge dam to generate electricity. The road would cut the saola's range in two, and the water rising behind the dam would drown almost all of the rivers in the lowlands. If something isn't done, the Lost World may be lost once again, only this time forever.

Fortunately, something is being done. When the saola was discovered, the outside world realized how important it was to save the Annamite Mountains. The government of Vietnam banned logging and hunting in the area, and enlarged the Vu Quang Nature Reserve from 40,000 acres (16,000 hectares) to almost 160,000 acres (65,000 hectares). In addition, the government of Laos set up the Nakai Nam Theun National Biodiversity Conservation Area on their side of the border, protecting 1,400 square miles (3,626 square kilometers) of forest.

Creating reserves on a map, though, does not stop poachers who cross from Vietnam into Laos to hunt. Nor does it stop loggers. Most of all, it does not stop poverty. Vu Quang is in the poorest part of Vietnam, and unless the people who live there can find other ways to get food and money, they will keep looking to the forest and to the animals in it. That is why scientists and conservationists are working with the governments of Laos and Vietnam, not just to save the animals of the Lost World, but also to help the people who live among them.

Maurizio Dioli

In 1981, Maurizio Dioli left his native Italy for northern Kenya, where he spent ten years studying camels. Besides journeying to Cambodia in search of the *kting voar*, his work has taken him through Africa from Namibia to Ethiopia, where today he directs a veterinary training program for the Red Cross.

Maurizio says he has "an everlasting and never tiring love for nature that allows [him] to see things where others see nothing." Besides the *kting voar*, he has discovered four new species of desert plant. One of them, *Aloe dioli*, was named after him in 1995.

Does the mysterious *linh duong* live on this forested hill in northeastern Cambodia?

Another set, found in 1929, turned up in the Kansas Museum of Natural History in the United States, misidentified as the horns of a kouprey, a rare Cambodian wild ox. Eastern Cambodia seemed the place to look for a living *Pseudonovibos spiralis*.

So Maurizio Dioli, a young Italian zoologist, went off to interview hunters in the remote forests of northeastern Cambodia.

The hunters told him about a rare black or gray buffalo-like animal that lives in small groups in the high, remote forests of Cambodia. They called it *kting voar*, "the wild cow with horns like lianas" (twisted forest vines), or *kting sipuoh*, "the wild cow that eats snakes." It's hard to imagine a cow eating snakes, but the hunters believed that the animal's horns, ground up and taken as medicine, could protect them against snakebite.

Dioli never found the animal. So what is *Pseudonovibos spiralis*?

In a Chinese encyclopedia printed almost 400 years ago, there is a drawing of an animal called a *ling*. The horns of the ling are twisted, like the horns of *Pseudonovibos spiralis*, and the encyclopedia says: "People in the south eat it to avoid snake and insect attacks." Is the ling really *Pseudonovibos*? It must be a very strange animal: the encyclopedia says that at night it hangs by its horns from a tree!

Whatever it is, *Pseudonovibos spiralis* must be endangered. Cambodia is a poor and war-torn country, not a safe place for rare animals. Cambodian hunters think that the animal may already be extinct in Vietnam. Unless we can find out more about *Pseudonovibos spiralis*, it could disappear, leaving us with nothing but horns and hunters' tales. I hope that we find it soon.

If *Pseudonovibos* becomes extinct, we may never know what the animals that grew these horns really looked like. Can we find it in time?

New Relations

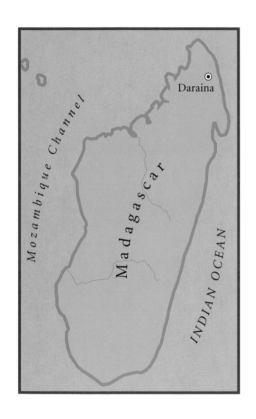

Daraina

Mozambique Channel

Madagascar

INDIAN OCEAN

ell me, pretty maiden," runs an old song, "are there any more at home like you?" "There are a few," goes the reply.

In the warmer forests of the world, there are more than a few like us. They are the other primates, our closest relatives: apes, monkeys, lemurs and their kind. We are still, much to our astonishment, discovering new primates today.

Most primates are fairly large animals. They are active by day and not hard to see, provided you're in the right place. Scientists have been crawling through the right sorts of places—rainforests mostly—for years, searching for primates. It's surprising to think we may have overlooked some.

But we did. In the past dozen years or so, scientists have discovered three new lemurs in Madagascar, at least six marmosets, a squirrel monkey and a capuchin monkey in South America, and the large, brightly colored sun-tailed guenon *(Cercopithecus solatus)* in Africa. In tropical Asia there may be as many as three new lorises (which look like lemurs) and a new tarsier (which resembles a miniature version of the creatures from the movie *Gremlins*).

A Rescue in the Rain

The Golden-crowned Sifaka *(Propithecus tattersalli)*

The rescue team from North Carolina's Duke University Primate Center arrived in northeastern Madagascar's remote Daraina Forest on November 22, 1987, in the middle of a violent rainstorm. At the time they didn't quite know what they were trying to rescue.

The story really starts 13 years earlier. In 1974, Ian Tattersall, a primate expert from New York's American Museum of Natural History, was visiting Daraina. Tattersall found a group of white lemurs with bright orange crowns capering through the forest. The local people called them *ankomba malandy*, which means "white lemur."

How Can You Help?

Would you like to help Duke University's Primate Center save Madagascar's endangered lemurs? You or your class could join Duke University's Adopt-a-Lemur Program. Find out how by writing to: Duke University Primate Center, 3705 Erwin Road, Durham, NC, 27705, U.S.A. Or visit their web site at http://www.duke.edu/web/primate/adopt.html. Every little bit helps.

Scientists at Duke University are hoping to save the golden-crowned sifaka, one of Madagascar's rarest lemurs, by breeding it in captivity.

The long arms and legs of the golden-crowned sifaka are ideal for leaping from tree to tree.

Tattersall thought the animals were diademed sifakas, beautiful long-legged, long-tailed lemurs famous for their great bounding leaps from tree to tree. He took some photographs and left.

There matters remained until 1986, when the Duke University Primate Center received some alarming news: the forest at Daraina was going to be clear-cut for charcoal. Dr. Tattersall's sifakas were doomed. Duke University sent a rescue team, but when they captured their first *ankomba malandy*, they got a big surprise. It was not a diademed sifaka after all.

First, the animal was too small. Also, its fur was short and its ears had long, furry tips, unlike any other sifaka. It was a new species. In 1988, Dr. Elwyn Simons of Duke University named it *Propithecus tattersalli*, in Ian Tattersall's honor. In English it is called the golden-crowned sifaka.

The team took two male and two female golden-crowned sifakas back to Duke University. In 1993, two more animals were brought from Madagascar to join them. Unfortunately, although two babies were born, neither is still alive. No more golden-crowned sifakas have been born, and only three of the animals remain at Duke University.

There may be no more than a few hundred golden-crowned sifakas left in the world. Their whole range is only about 15 miles (24 kilometers) across. Not all of that is forest, and none of it is protected. The forests near Daraina are shrinking every year. People continue to cut down the trees that the golden-crowned sifaka needs to survive. Even worse, there may be gold in Daraina's soil, and because Madagascar is a poor country, its government is not eager to protect Daraina when it could earn money instead. Gold miners invading the area are hunting the golden-crowned sifaka for food. The ankomba malandy is in a race against time.

The Cyanide Eater

The Golden Bamboo Lemur *(Hapalemur aureus)*

Plants can't run away if something wants to eat them. Instead, they defend themselves with thorns, barbs or poisons. One of the best-defended plants on earth is the giant bamboo, *Cephalostachyum viguieri*, of the rainforests of eastern Madagascar. Its tender growing tips, the parts a hungry animal would be most eager to eat, are laced with cyanide, a deadly poison.

In 1985, scientists were astonished to discover that one animal, weighing only a little over 3 pounds (1.4 kilograms), eats around 17.5 ounces (500 grams) of giant bamboo every day. That's enough to kill a human being.

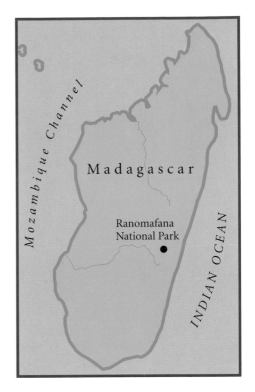

A golden bamboo lemur in the wild in Ranomafana National Park, Madagasacar.

The shoots of giant bamboo that a golden bamboo lemur eats every day contain enough cyanide to kill a human being.

How Can You Help?

Help protect Ranomafana National Park by buying a poster of the golden bamboo lemur. Order your poster by writing a letter and mailing it, with a check or money order, to: The Institute for the Conservation of Tropical Environments (ICTE), SBS Building, 5th Floor, State University of New York at Stony Brook, Stony Brook, NY, 11794-4364, U.S.A. It costs only US$7.00.

The animal is the golden bamboo lemur *(Hapalemur aureus)*, and it doesn't just eat bamboo tips now and again: it eats little else. That may seem pretty risky, but there's a good reason for it. The golden bamboo lemur shares the forest of Ranomafana National Park, Madagascar, with its two cousins: the greater bamboo lemur *(Hapalemur simus)* and the gentle bamboo lemur *(Hapalemur griseus)*. All three eat bamboo. So what keeps them from fighting over the same meal?

The answer? The golden bamboo lemur eats the shoots, leaves, pith and viny parts of the giant bamboo. The greater bamboo lemur eats giant bamboo too but usually concentrates only on the mature stalks, while the gentle bamboo lemur eats another kind of bamboo entirely. In this way the three species manage to stay out of each other's fur, so to speak. The bamboo that the gentle bamboo lemur eats has no cyanide in it; neither do the mature stalks the greater bamboo lemur prefers. Only the golden bamboo lemur ends up with the poisonous bits, and in order to survive it has developed a way to digest a food that would kill a dozen of its cousins.

How does the golden bamboo lemur do it? We don't know for sure, but we do know that the golden bamboo lemur (and some other lemurs too) regularly climbs down from the trees to eat soil. Scientists suspect that there are chemicals in the soil that act as an antidote to the cyanide and help the golden bamboo lemur digest its poisonous meal. If this is true, the golden bamboo lemur's secret may be as simple as eating the right kind of dirt.

However, it wasn't until zoologists Patricia Wright and Bernhard Meier spotted a lemur they couldn't identify at Ranomafana National Park in 1986 that scientists had any idea this was going on. Wright and Meier soon confirmed that the golden bamboo lemur was a new species. As well as being new, this lemur is also very rare, and the forests in the park where it lives are threatened. Not only is the golden bamboo lemur a most fascinating species, it is also one of the most endangered.

Madagascar

There is no place on earth like Madagascar. Most of its animals, and many of its plants, are found nowhere else in the world. It has tomato-red frogs, giant chameleons, horn-nosed snakes, and, especially, lemurs: 33 species of them. Except for some nearby islands, not one is found anywhere else.

Sadly, Madagascar's wildlife is the most endangered on earth. Almost all of its wild habitats have been destroyed. Its people, among the poorest on earth, are cutting and burning much of the rest. Today, scientists from around the world are racing to help the people of Madagascar save what is left of its wonderful plants and animals.

The Fisherman's Monkey

The Black-faced Lion Tamarin
(Leontopithecus caissara)

Clinging to the coast of Brazil, 930 miles (1,500 kilometers) south of the Amazon, is one of the most endangered rainforests in the world. It is called *mata Atlantica*, the Atlantic forest. At one time it was two and a half times the size of California, but today almost 95 percent of it has been destroyed.

The black-faced lion tamarin may be the rarest primate in South America. It was not discovered until 1990.

There are still pockets of Atlantic forest left. In February 1990, Brazilian zoologists Maria Lucia Lorini and Vanessa Guerra Persson traveled to one of them—the 34,580-acre (14,000-hectare) island of Superagüi, only 155 miles (250 kilometers) south of Brazil's largest city, São Paulo. What, they wanted to know, lay behind islanders' tales, some over a century old, of a *sagüi*, a "little monkey?"

Almost as soon as they arrived, a *caiçara*, or "local fisherman," presented the zoologists with the body of a squirrel-sized, golden-furred creature with black face, tail and forearms. It was a new species of lion tamarin.

Lorini and Persson were already familiar with lion tamarins. There were three species of these rare, tiny, brightly colored, shaggy-maned primates living in small patches of Atlantic forest several hundred kilometers to the north of

The Saterê marmoset is well-known to local people in the Amazon, who call it the "zip"— but scientists did not find it until 1996.

Amazon Surprises

The Rio Maués marmoset was one of three new species of primate discovered in the Amazon forests in 1992.

Since 1990, at least six new monkeys have been discovered in Brazil.

That's not really surprising. Over 75 of the world's 250 or so known primate species live in Brazil, most of them in its Amazon rainforests. There are areas of Amazonia that primatologists, the scientists who study primates, have yet to explore.

In 1992, scientists named three new monkeys: the Ka'apor capuchin (*Cebus kaapori*), the Rio Maués marmoset (*Callithrix mauesi*) and the black-headed marmoset (*Callithrix nigriceps*). Marmosets, like their cousins the tamarins, are no bigger than squirrels. They usually live in family groups. Only a single female in the group has babies, usually twins, but the whole group takes care of them.

Another marmoset, *Callithrix marcai*, was described in 1995; and yet another, the Saterê marmoset (*Callithrix saterei*), in 1996. The Saterê marmoset must move very quickly:

the local people call it "zip." In 1994, José de Sousa e Silva Jr. and Mauricio de Almeida e Noronha heard stories of the "zip" and set off to find it. The people who knew most about it, though, were poachers, and they were not eager to help scientists. Finally, the scientists heard of a man who had a "zip" as a pet. When they went to visit, he came out to greet them with the "zip" sitting on his head!

In 1996, a man holding a tin can showed up at Marc Van Roosmalen's primate orphanage in Manaus, a city in the heart of Amazon. Nestled inside was a greenish-gray marmoset no bigger than a mouse. As soon as Van Roosmalen saw it, only 4 inches (10.2 centimeters) long, with a black crown and a white fringe framing its face, he knew it was something new. In fact it was the second-smallest monkey in the world! Van Roosmalen christened his discovery the dwarf marmoset (*Callithrix humilis*).

It took Van Roosmalen over a year to track down more dwarf

The adult dwarf marmoset does not have as much white on its head as a young animal.

marmosets. He found them living along the western bank of the Rio Aripuanã, a large tributary of the

This young dwarf marmoset does not appreciate being held by its discoverer, Marc Van Roosmalen.

Amazon. They live in the smallest range of any Amazonian primate and are the only marmosets that do not defend their territory against their own kind.

The Amazon still has not revealed all of its monkey surprises. Van Roosmalen has found at least three more monkeys that could turn out to be new species, and he thinks there may be more waiting to be described.

Finding these animals may be very important. The rainforests are being destroyed by settlers, loggers, cattle ranchers, gold miners and others. The Ka'apor capuchin and the black-headed marmoset are already in danger. But to protect the rare animals of the Amazon, we first have to know what, and where, they are. If we don't find all of Brazil's monkeys soon, some could vanish before we even know they are there.

Superagüi. The fisherman's prize, the fourth lion tamarin, is the rarest of all. It is probably the most endangered primate in the New World. Lorini and Persson named it *Leontopithecus caissara*, after the fisherman who gave them their first specimen (and helped them search for living tamarins). The local fishermen call it *cara-preta*, or "black-face," and from that name comes the English version, the black-faced lion tamarin.

A few months later, Lorini and Persson joined a special project to find out more about the black-faced lion tamarin's situation. There are probably only about 260 left in the world. They live in about 50 family groups on Superagüi and in several places on the nearby mainland.

Superagüi is close to a popular resort area. Its beautiful sandy beaches attract sun-worshiping tourists and money-worshiping developers. The black-faced lion tamarins prefer a special kind of scrubby forest, called restinga, that grows right behind these sandy beaches, in just the sort of places that developers like to put hotels and golf courses.

Recently, things have improved for the black-faced lion tamarin. In November 1997, the Brazilian government expanded a national park on Superagüi from 52,900 to 84,600 acres (21,400 to 34,254 hectares). The new land protects the habitat of some of the most important tamarin populations. Now and again tamarins are still caught and sold as pets, though this practice is illegal. The land where they live outside of the park continues to be farmed, logged and developed. In the newly expanded park, however, the black-faced lion tamarin has a real chance for survival.

Out of the Sea

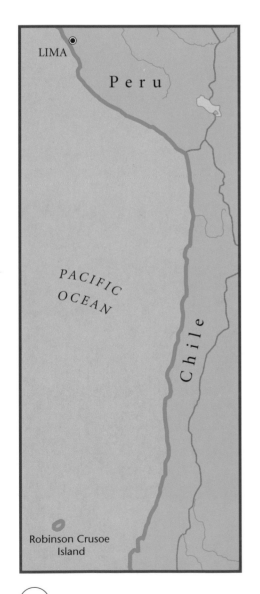

LIMA

Peru

PACIFIC OCEAN

Chile

Robinson Crusoe Island

f you want to discover *really* unknown animals—creatures never before seen by human eyes—the place to look is in the sea. The ocean's depths have concealed whole worlds. In 1977, a deep-sea submersible a mile and a half (2.4 kilometers) down in the eastern Pacific found masses of clams bigger than your head, 6-foot-long (1.8-meter-long) worms with bright red gills poking out of white, parchment-like tubes, and a host of other bizarre creatures, all clustered around a volcanic vent in the ocean floor. In 2000, Australian scientists announced that they had discovered hundreds of new species living on underwater mountains. These species are called *seamounts*. Some belonged to groups of animals thought to be extinct for 65 million years!

Vent animals live in a universe of their own. Most living things take energy from the sun (in a process called photosynthesis) or eat other things that do. Vent animals, by contrast, are part of a separate food chain. This chain is not based on energy from the sun, but on bacteria that draw energy from volcanic chemicals oozing through a vent beneath the ocean's floor.

We now know that vent animals live in many places in the deep, dark sea, but we have little idea of what else may share those depths.

That includes that fearsome monster, the giant squid. From time to time over the last 100 years, dying squid floundering on the ocean's surface have given fishermen the scare of their lives. The bodies of dead squid have been found washed up on shore. But no one has ever seen a healthy giant squid in its home at the bottom of the sea.

Maybe you'll be the first. If you are, be careful!

Two New Whales—Or Is It Three?

The Pygmy Beaked Whale
(*Mesoplodon peruvianus*)—And More?

How can you overlook a whale?

The ocean is so huge (ships can cover only a small part of it) that sometimes even a whale can be hard to find. That is

This adult male pygmy beaked whale, carrying the scars of combats with rival males, was drawn by Julio Reyes, one of its discoverers.

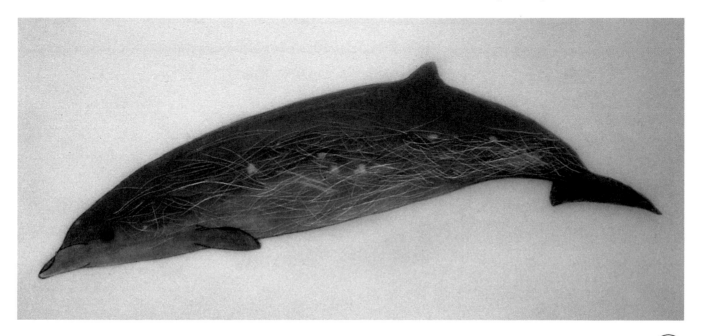

Julio Reyes

Julio Reyes was born in Lima, Peru in 1958. One day he found a porpoise in a fish market. Ever since then, he has devoted himself to studying Peru's whales and dolphins, and helping to save them from extinction.

In 1985, he joined an international project to save Burmeister's porpoise, a small South American whale that is caught for human consumption and crab bait. He has also studied the biology and conservation status of Peru's other whale species, and has published several articles about them.

why we know practically nothing about most beaked whales.

Beaked whales look like oversized dolphins. But while dolphins can be curious and playful, beaked whales are shy and quiet. They stay far out to sea, away from the traffic of shipping lanes. One species of beaked whale, Longman's beaked whale *(Indopacetus pacificus)*, is known only from two skulls that were found washed up on beaches in Australia and Tanzania.

In 1976, Dr. James Mead was visiting a fish market in Peru. He found part of a beaked whale skull he couldn't recognize. It took another nine years before Peruvian scientist Julio Reyes found another skull, in another fish market. However, there still wasn't enough of the specimen to identify the species.

A few months later a dead female washed ashore on a Peruvian beach, and over the next few years at least six more were found drowned in the drift nets Peruvian fishermen set for sharks.

Reyes, Mead and Belgian scientist Koen Van Waerebeek now knew enough about the species to give their new whale a name. They called it *Mesoplodon peruvianus*, the pygmy beaked whale. For the description, they had to write three pages of detailed tooth and skull measurements to prove that their whale was new.

Today we know that the pygmy beaked whale, the smallest known beaked whale at only 12.1 feet (3.7 meters) in length, can be found at least as far north as Baja California in Mexico. Groups of two or three pygmy beaked whales have been seen at sea. We also know it eats fish and squid. And that's about all we know!

There is another mysterious beaked whale that lives in the same waters off South America. It has been sighted at least 30 times over the past 10 years, in groups of up to eight animals. One was seen jumping three times in a row. The animal is more striking than the pygmy beaked whale. The larger animals, probably the males, have a broad band of white, like a pale cape, over the tops of their bodies. Scientists call it *Mesoplodon* species "A." They cannot name it because they do not have a specimen—or do they?

In 1997, Reyes, Van Waerebeek and two Chilean scientists, Juan Carlos Cárdenas and José Yañez, described a skull found on Robinson Crusoe Island, Chile, as another new species of beaked whale. They named it Bahamonde's beaked whale *(Mesoplodon bahamondi).* Is this the mysterious species "A"? Is it just an oddly shaped skull from a species we already know? Could there be three new beaked whales in South America: the pygmy, Bahamonde's and species "A"? Nobody knows—yet!

Some beaked whales are very strange-looking. The male Blainville's beaked whale (*Mesoplodon densirostris*), shown here, has only two teeth, carried like horns on high ridges of its lower jaw.

And Now for Something Completely Different

The Loriciferans and Their Neighbors

How would you like to hold 10,000 animals in one hand, including some species unknown to science?

Well, you can. The next time you go to a seaside beach, walk down to the waterline and pick up a handful of wet sand. It will be filled with animals so small, they cling to the sand grains and even swim between them like divers around mounds of coral. They come in outlandish shapes and have even more bizarre names: gastrotrichs, kinorhynchs, tardigrades.

Phylum

Scientists have named only about 35 animal *phyla* (the plural of phylum). A phylum is a major group of animals that have bodies organized in the same basic way. An octopus and an oyster may seem very different, but they belong to the same phylum, Mollusca. On the other hand, caterpillars and earthworms look somewhat alike, but they belong to different phyla. You and I belong to the same phylum—Chordata—as fish do, because we both share a nerve cord that runs down our backs. Insect nerve cords run along their undersides, and some animals don't even have them.

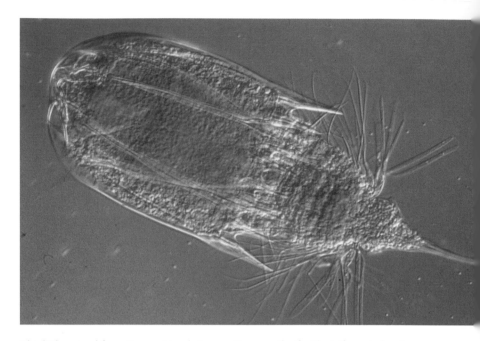

This little animal from France, *Nanoloricus mysticus,* was the first loriciferan to be given a scientific name.

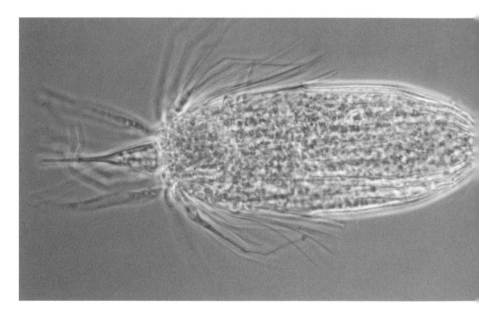

Pliciloricus gracilis is one of over 70 known species in the Loricifera, a phylum of animals no one had even seen before 1974.

These are the meiofauna (pronounced *my'-oh-faw*-na), meaning "lesser animals." Scientists are only just beginning to understand the universe of sand where they live. The meiofauna are nature's cleanup crew. They eat the bits of decaying animal and plant matter that, if left to rot, would soon turn a beautiful beach into a stinking mess.

For years, Dr. Reinhardt Møbjerg Kristensen, a Danish expert on the meiofauna, had been finding strange microscopic animals in the sands of Denmark, Greenland and even the Coral Sea. When he showed his finds to Dr. Robert Higgins, a scientist who has been studying the meiofauna for 40 years, Higgins recognized them as the same sort of puzzling animal he had found off the coast of South Carolina in 1974.

These creatures were not just new species; they were a whole new kind of animal! Their bodies are made up of the smallest cells in the animal kingdom. They had to be put into a brand-new phylum. For an animal to be so different that it requires a new phylum, it has to be pretty unusual.

These new animals certainly are unusual. Imagine a microscopic eggshell with one end broken off. Sticking out of the broken end is a loose puffball with up to 200 tentacles, and out of that sticks a sharp, pointed beak. Now imagine that the animal can pull that beak and puffball (or, to be precise, its head and thorax) back into the eggshell. If you can picture that, you'll have some idea what these strange animals look like.

The "beak" is really a collection of spiky mouthparts, and the "eggshell" is a set of six plates linked together like a girdle (what women wear to hold their stomachs in). Dr. Kristensen called the new phylum *Loricifera* (pronounced *lore-ih-siff'-er-ah*), which means "girdle-wearers." The first species he named—the type species of the new phylum—was *Nanoloricus mysticus*, "the strange little girdle."

Scientists have already discovered and named more than 70 species of loriciferan, and more are on the way. Several

Dr. Reinhardt Møbjerg Kristensen

Dr. Reinhardt Møbjerg Kristensen, a professor at the Museum of Zoology in Copenhagen, Denmark, has searched for meiofauna from Greenland to New Zealand. One of his newest discoveries is a microscopic animal discovered in a cold spring in West Greenland. It has very complicated jaws and armor plates on its back. It is so unusual that it, too, belongs in a new phylum—the third that Dr. Kristensen has discovered!

have turned up around Antarctica and some 5 miles (8 kilometers) down in the South Pacific Ocean. But scientists have yet to see a live adult loriciferan. You see, the only way to remove them from the sand is to flush them out with fresh water, and this kills them. So we don't know how loriciferans eat or how they find mates (though we do know that the females lay eggs that are almost *half* their size). We don't even know how they move.

What we *do* know is that, although we didn't see a loriciferan before 1974, the world is full of them. And if we didn't know about *them*, how much do we really know about the environment that we, and the loriciferans, share?

The Hidden Life of Seafood

Symbion pandora and the Cycliophora

Naming one new phylum should be enough excitement for any scientist. But in 1995, Dr. Kristensen helped name a *second* one.

If you've ever eaten scampi—the fancy name for Norway lobsters *(Nephrops norvegicus)*—you were actually eating the home of *Symbion pandora*, one of the strangest animals on earth. *Symbion pandora* is smaller than the period at the end of this sentence. Even under a microscope it doesn't look like much, resembling a badly stuffed sock with a sucker at one end. That sucker clings to the bristles on the Norway lobster's lips. On the other end there is a funnel edged with a fringe of tiny hairlike projections called cilia. The waving cilia create currents in the water that draw bits of food dropped from the lobster's lips into *Symbion pandora*'s mouth. The cilia's regular movement (sort of like the "wave" at a baseball game) makes

The only home of *Symbion pandora*: a Norway lobster.

the funnel look like a spinning wheel. Peter Funch and Dr. Kristensen had to create a new phylum for this strange creature. They called it *Cycliophora* (pronounced *sick-lee-aw'-for-ah*), or "wheel mouths."

Because these creatures only live clustered on the Norway lobster's lips, Funch and Kristensen named them *Symbion*, which means "living together." Pandora, according to the ancient Greeks, was the first woman. The gods gave her a magic box, warning her never to open it. When she ignored their warning and opened it anyway, she released all the evil in the world. *Symbion pandora* reminded Funch and Kristensen of a box full of mysteries. Instead of containing evils, however, inside *Symbion pandora* (and this is what makes it such a weird

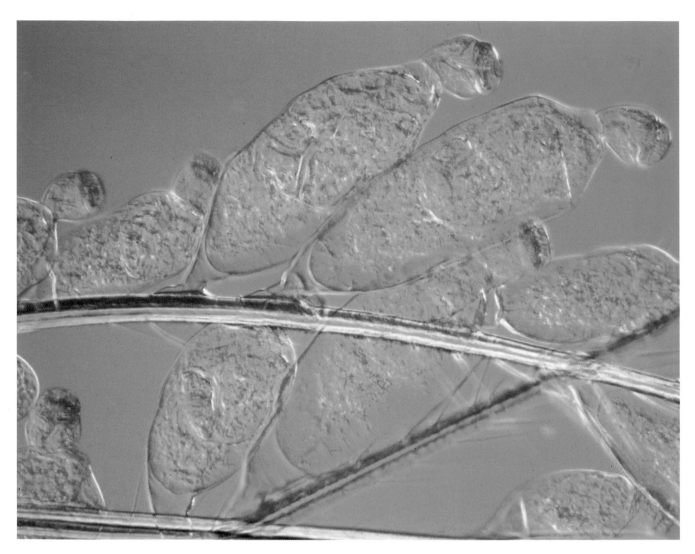

A cluster of *Symbion pandora* clings to a bristle of a Norway lobster. *Symbion* is the only known member of a new animal phylum, the Cycliophora.

little animal) there are copies of itself. Here's how we think it works.

The animal clinging to the lobster's bristles is neither male nor female; it is called a *feeding stage*. This is the only time in its life cycle that *Symbion pandora* eats. As the feeding stage grows, a bud develops inside its body. Eventually the bud emerges and becomes a new funnel, with a new mouth attached to a new digestive tract. The old funnel and digestive tract wither away. Imagine growing a new head inside your body, attached to a new stomach. When your new head pops out, your old head and your old stomach wither and disappear.

Now imagine doing this several times as you grow up—and that's what we think *Symbion pandora* does.

After this process happens a few times, one of the buds eventually becomes not a funnel but a larva, which escapes and settles down on a nearby bristle to grow into a brand-new feeding stage. This could go on and on, except for one problem: the larva can't swim. That means it can't hop over to a new lobster once the lobster sheds its skin.

So, every once in a while, just before the lobster sheds, some of the feeding stages grow different, special buds. Some are female, others are male. The males fertilize the females, and the larvae that are produced can swim. The larvae break out of the female's body, swim off to find a new lobster, settle down and grow into a new feeding stage, and the cycle starts again. Sound complicated? It is!

How many more amazing finds await us in the most ordinary places? As Dr. Simon Conway Morris put it in the journal *Nature*, where the discovery of *Symbion pandora* was announced: "Next time you are at your favorite seafood restaurant, make sure the waiter has a couple of zoology textbooks and a decent microscope on the pudding trolley. Who knows what might be found lurking under the lettuce?"

Now What?

Saving New Species

any of the animals in this book are in danger of extinction. Discovering them may help to save them, because it is hard to protect something if you don't know it exists. In 1997, Marcos Bornschein and Bianca Reinert discovered a tiny bird, the Wet Tall-grass Tapaculo *(Scytalopus iraiensis)*, near Curitiba in Brazil—just as its home was due to be flooded by a dam. The bird might have been wiped out before we knew anything about it, but now Bornschein and Reinert are mounting a worldwide campaign to stop the dam and save the Wet Tall-grass Tapaculo from extinction.

Unfortunately, discovery has its bad side too. Some people make money catching and selling endangered species, even though it's against the law. Announcing a discovery actually helps these fortune hunters, by letting them know that there is something new worth hunting. Now, scientists try to make sure a new species is safe from fortune hunters before telling the world about it.

When a new species does make headlines, though, the publicity can help conservationists convince local governments to protect the animal's habitat. Knowing about the golden bamboo lemur may make it easier to protect Ranomafana National Park in Madagascar, and knowing about the black-faced lion tamarin is helping save the island of Superagüi in Brazil. And Vietnam is working hard to protect the Vu Quang forests where the saola lives.

In 1991, scientists agreed to name the Choco vireo, a new bird from Colombia, South America, after whoever would supply $50,000 towards its conservation. A man named Bernard Master donated the money to Birdlife International, and the bird has been named *Vireo masteri* in his honor. The donation will help protect the Rio Nambi Community Nature Reserve, where the vireo lives with over 300 other bird species, including eight endangered ones.

Discovery can make a difference!

What Else Is Out There?

For years there have been stories about strange creatures lurking in forests, at the bottom of lakes and in the depths of the sea. Are we about to find Bigfoot? The Loch Ness monster? Yeti, the abominable snowman? Or *mkole-mbembe*, the "dinosaur" that supposedly lives in central Africa? After all, if the saola exists, why can't they?

Cryptozoology is the study of these "hidden" animals. Many cryptozoologists believe it is only a matter of time before some of these animals are discovered. Most scientists do not take these stories seriously and I think the scientists are probably right. Remember that scientists found the saola specimens first and heard the stories afterwards. That is how most real animals are discovered. We have no specimens of Bigfoot or "Nessie," and they are probably no more real than the unicorn.

Of course, I would love to be wrong. There is a chance that some of the "hidden" animals, especially the ones in the oceans, could turn out to be real. *Mesoplodon* species "A" certainly exists, even though we have no specimen.

But even if there aren't any dinosaurs in Africa or ape-men in China, there are still millions of new species waiting to be discovered. Most of them will be small, but a few may be large and, in the oceans at least, even huge. When we do finally discover them, they will probably come as a complete surprise. They will be, unlike Bigfoot or the Loch Ness monster, creatures we had never even imagined before.

What could be more exciting than that?

Though there are no specimens or photographs of *Mesoplodon* species "A", we do know it exists. It may look something like this female Blainville's Beaked Whale (*Mesoplodon densirostris*).

Index